Bride Groom

Wedding Date:

This Wedding Planner Belongs To:

Brides Parents

Mother of the Bride _____

Father of the Bride _____

Grooms Parents

Mother of the Groom _____

Father of the Groom _____

Plans & Ideas

Thoughts

IDEAS FOR THEME

IDEAS FOR VENUE

IDEAS FOR COLORS

IDEAS FOR MUSIC

IDEAS FOR RECEPTION

OTHER IDEAS

Plans & Ideas

Must Haves

Important Dates

DATE:	DATE: June 7	DATE: June 19-22	REMINDERS
	Bridal Shower	Bachelorette	Invites for shower
			Cake/Desserts
DATE:	DATE:	DATE:	
DATE:	DATE:	DATE:	NOTES
DATE:	DATE:	DATE:	
DATE:	DATE:	DATE:	

Important Dates

DATE:	DATE:	DATE:	REMINDERS
DATE:	DATE:	DATE:	
DATE:	DATE:	DATE:	NOTES
DATE:	DATE:	DATE:	
DATE:	DATE:	DATE:	

Wedding Budget
Expense MANAGER

CATEGORY/ITEMS	BUDGET	ACTUAL COST	BALANCE

Wedding Budget Checklist

CATEGORY	BUDGET	ACTUAL COST	DEPOSIT	BALANCE

Notes

Notes

Travel Plans

PARENTS TRAVEL EXPENSE TRACKER

	BUDGET	COST	DEPOSIT	BALANCE	DUE DATE
TRAVEL PLANS					
AIRLINE					
HOTEL					
CAR RENTAL					

NOTES & *Reminders*

SPECIAL REMINDERS

Travel Plans

PARENTS TRAVEL EXPENSE TRACKER

	BUDGET	COST	DEPOSIT	BALANCE	DUE DATE
TRAVEL PLANS					
AIRLINE					
HOTEL					
CAR RENTAL					

NOTES & Reminders

SPECIAL REMINDERS

Notes

Rehearsal Dinner Plans

 Rehearsal Dinner Guests

NAME	ADDRESS	PHONE#	# IN PARTY	RSVP ✓

 # Rehearsal Dinner Guests

NAME	ADDRESS	PHONE#	# IN PARTY	RSVP ✓

Bridal Shower Plans

Bridal Shower Budget

CATEGORY	BUDGET	ACTUAL COST	DEPOSIT	BALANCE
Venue	$500	500	$200	
Food	200			
Beverage	300			
Decorations	100			

 # Bridal Shower Guests

NAME	ADDRESS	PHONE#	# IN PARTY	RSVP ✓

 # Bridal Shower Guests

NAME	ADDRESS	PHONE#	# IN PARTY	RSVP ✓

Honeymoon Plans & Ideas

Dreams

Wedding Planner
PLANNING GUIDELINE
12 Months BEFORE WEDDING

- [x] SET THE DATE
- [x] SET YOUR BUDGET
- [ ] CONSIDER WEDDING THEMES
- [x] PLAN ENGAGEMENT PARTY
- [x] RESEARCH POSSIBLE VENUES
- [x] START RESEARCHING GOWNS
- [x] RESEARCH PHOTOGRAPHERS
- [ ] RESEARCH VIDEOGRAPHERS
- [x] RESEARCH DJ'S/ENTERTAINMENT

- [ ] CONSIDER FLORISTS
- [x] RESEARCH CATERERS
- [ ] DECIDE ON OFFICIANT
- [x] CREATE INITIAL GUEST LIST
- [x] CHOOSE WEDDING PARTY
- [ ] CONSIDER ACCESSORIES
- [x] REGISTER WITH GIFT REGISTRY
- [ ] DISCUSS HONEYMOON IDEAS
- [ ] RESEARCH WEDDING RINGS — *Carter's ring*

- [ ] CONSIDER MUSIC CHOICES
- [ ] CONSIDER CAKE BAKER
- [ ] CONSIDER TRANSPORTATION
- [x] CHOOSE MENU
- [ ] BOOK A WEDDING PLANNER
- [ ] BRIDESMAIDS GOWNS — *ordered?*
- [ ] BOOK TENTATIVE HOTELS
- [ ] CONSIDER BEAUTY SALONS
- [ ] CONSIDER SHOES & OTHER

Things To Do | Status

- Cake (for cutting)
- Desserts
- Hair
- Makeup

TOP PRIORITIES

NOTES & IDEAS

APPOINTMENTS & REMINDERS

Wedding Contact List

IMPORTANT VENDOR CONTACTS

	NAME	PHONE #	EMAIL	ADDRESS
OFFICIANT	Kerry			
RECEPTION VENUE	The Hive			
BRIDAL SHOP				
SEAMSTRESS				
FLORIST				
CATERER	Coco/Nimis			
DJ/ENTERTAINMENT	MicDrop			
WEDDING VENUE	The Hive			
TRANSPORTATION				
OTHER:				
OTHER:				
OTHER:				

Notes

SPECIAL REMINDERS

Planning Snapshot

CEREMONY EXPENSE TRACKER

	BUDGET	COST	DEPOSIT	BALANCE	DUE DATE
OFFICIANT GRATUITY					
MARRIAGE LICENSE					
VENUE COST					
FLOWERS					
DECORATIONS					
OTHER					

NOTES & Reminders

NOTES & REMINDERS

RECEPTION EXPENSE TRACKER

	BUDGET	COST	DEPOSIT	BALANCE	DUE DATE
VENUE FEE					
CATERING/FOOD					
BAR/BEVERAGES					
CAKE/CUTTING FEE					
DECORATIONS					
RENTALS/EXTRAS					
BARTENDER/STAFF					

NOTES & More

SPECIAL REMINDERS

Planning Snapshot

PAPER PRODUCTS EXPENSE TRACKER

	BUDGET	COST	DEPOSIT	BALANCE	DUE DATE
INVITATIONS/CARDS					
POSTAGE COSTS					
THANK YOU CARDS					
PLACE CARDS					
GUESTBOOK					
OTHER					

NOTES & *Reminders*

NOTES & REMINDERS

ENTERTAINMENT EXPENSE TRACKER

	BUDGET	COST	DEPOSIT	BALANCE	DUE DATE
BAND/DJ					
SOUND SYSTEM RENTAL					
VENUE/DANCE RENTAL					
GRATUITIES					
OTHER:					
OTHER:					
OTHER:					

NOTES & *More*

SPECIAL REMINDERS

Planning Snapshot

WEDDING PARTY ATTIRE EXPENSE TRACKER

	BUDGET	COST	DEPOSIT	BALANCE	DUE DATE
WEDDING DRESS		3500		Pd	
TUX RENTALS					
BRIDESMAID DRESSES					
SHOES/HEELS					
VEIL/GARTER/OTHER					
ALTERATION COSTS					

NOTES & Reminders

NOTES & REMINDERS

TRANSPORTATION EXPENSE TRACKER

	BUDGET	COST	DEPOSIT	BALANCE	DUE DATE
LIMO RENTAL					
VALET PARKING					
VENUE TRANSPORTATION					
AIRPORT TRANSPORTATION					
OTHER:					
OTHER:					
OTHER:					

NOTES & More

SPECIAL REMINDERS

Wedding Attire Planner

WEDDING ATTIRE EXPENSE TRACKER

ITEM/PURCHASE	STATUS ✓	DATE PAID	TOTAL COST
☐			
☐			
☐			
☐			
☐			

NOTES & REMINDERS

TOTAL COST:

Notes:

Wedding Attire Details

Wedding Attire Planner

MOTHER/FATHER OF THE BRIDE WEDDING ATTIRE EXPENSE TRACKER

	BUDGET	COST	DEPOSIT	BALANCE	DUE DATE
WEDDING ATTIRE	400				
SHOES/HEELS	150				
TUX RENTAL					
SUIT	150				
SHOES					
ALTERATION COSTS					

NOTES & Reminders

SPECIAL REMINDERS

Notes:

Wedding Attire Details

Planning Snapshot

FLORIST EXPENSE TRACKER

	BUDGET	COST	DEPOSIT	BALANCE	DUE DATE
BOUQUETS					
VENUE DECORATIONS					
BOUTONNIERES					
VASES/EXTRAS					
TABLE DECORATIONS					
OTHER:					

NOTES & Reminders

NOTES & REMINDERS

OTHER EXPENSE TRACKER

	BUDGET	COST	DEPOSIT	BALANCE	DUE DATE
PHOTOGRAPHER					
VIDEOGRAPHER					
CATERER					
HAIR/MAKEUP/SALON					
WEDDING RINGS					
WEDDING PARTY GIFTS					
OTHER:					

NOTES & More

SPECIAL REMINDERS

Florist Planner

FLORIST EXPENSE TRACKER

ITEM/PURCHASE	STATUS ✓	DATE PAID	TOTAL COST
☐			
☐			
☐			
☐			
☐			

NOTES & REMINDERS

TOTAL COST:

Notes:

Florist Planning Details

Venue Planner

VENUE EXPENSE TRACKER

ITEM/PURCHASE	STATUS ✓	DATE PAID	TOTAL COST
☐			
☐			
☐			
☐			
☐			

NOTES & REMINDERS

TOTAL COST:

Notes:

Venue Planning Details

Catering Planner

CATERING EXPENSE TRACKER

ITEM/PURCHASE	STATUS ✓	DATE PAID	TOTAL COST
☐			
☐			
☐			
☐			
☐			

NOTES & REMINDERS

TOTAL COST:

Notes:

Caterer Planner Details

Entertainment Planner

ITEM/PURCHASE	STATUS ✓	DATE PAID	TOTAL COST
☐			
☐			
☐			
☐			
☐			

ENTERTAINMENT EXPENSE TRACKER

NOTES & REMINDERS

TOTAL COST:

Notes:

Love

Entertainment Details

Videographer Planner

VIDEOGRAPHER EXPENSE TRACKER

ITEM/PURCHASE	STATUS ✓	DATE PAID	TOTAL COST
☐			
☐			
☐			
☐			
☐			

NOTES & REMINDERS

TOTAL COST:

Notes:

Videographer Details

Photographer Planner

ITEM/PURCHASE	STATUS ✓	DATE PAID	TOTAL COST
☐			
☐			
☐			
☐			
☐			

PHOTOGRAPHER EXPENSE TRACKER

NOTES & REMINDERS

TOTAL COST:

Notes:

Photographer Details

Extra Wedding Costs

MISC WEDDING EXPENSE TRACKER

ITEM/PURCHASE	STATUS ✓	DATE PAID	TOTAL COST
☐			
☐			
☐			
☐			
☐			

NOTES & REMINDERS

TOTAL COST:

Notes:

Misc Wedding Details

Bachelorette Party Planner

EVENT DETAILS

DATE: June 19-21
TIME:
VENUE: Chicago
THEME:
HOST: Wya Sutton
OTHER:

GUEST LIST

FIRST NAME	LAST NAME	✓

SCHEDULE OF EVENTS

TIME	
6/20	1:30 Cubs Game

SUPPLIES & SHOPPING LIST

- [ ]
- [ ]
- [ ]
- [ ]
- [ ]
- [ ]
- [ ]
- [ ]
- [ ]
- [ ]
- [ ]
- [ ]
- [ ]
- [ ]
- [ ]
- [ ]
- [ ]
- [ ]

NOTES & REMINDERS

love

Notes

Reception Planner

MEAL PLANNER IDEAS

HORS D'OEUVRES

1st COURSE:

3rd COURSE:

2nd COURSE:

4th COURSE:

Meal Planning Notes

Reception Planning Notes

IDEAS & REMINDERS

Bride's Planner

HAIR APPOINTMENT

SALON NAME	DATE	TIME	BOOKED FOR:	ADDRESS:
			☐ ☐ ☐	

NOTES	

MAKEUP APPOINTMENT

SALON NAME	DATE	TIME	BOOKED FOR:	ADDRESS:
			☐ ☐ ☐	

NOTES	

MANICURE/PEDICURE APPOINTMENT

SALON NAME	DATE	TIME	BOOKED FOR:	ADDRESS:
			☐	
			☐	
			☐	

NOTES	

Notes

Wedding Planner
PLANNING GUIDELINE

9 Months BEFORE WEDDING

- [x] FINALIZE GUEST LIST
- [x] ORDER INVITATIONS
- [x] PLAN YOUR RECEPTION
- [x] BOOK PHOTOGRAPHER
- [ ] BOOK VIDEOGRAPHER
- [x] CHOOSE WEDDING GOWN

- [ ] ORDER BRIDESMAIDS DRESSES
- [ ] RESERVE TUXEDOS
- [ ] ARRANGE TRANSPORTATION
- [x] BOOK WEDDING VENUE
- [x] BOOK RECEPTION VENUE
- [ ] PLAN HONEYMOON

- [ ] BOOK FLORIST
- [x] BOOK DJ/ENTERTAINMENT
- [x] BOOK CATERER
- [ ] CHOOSE WEDDING CAKE
- [x] BOOK OFFICIANT
- [ ] BOOK ROOMS FOR GUESTS

Things To Do	Status

TOP PRIORITIES

NOTES & IDEAS

APPOINTMENTS & REMINDERS

Wedding Planner
PLANNING GUIDELINE
6 Months
BEFORE WEDDING

- [ ] ORDER THANK YOU NOTES
- [ ] REVIEW RECEPTION DETAILS
- [ ] MAKE APPT FOR FITTING
- [ ] CONFIRM BRIDAL DRESSES
- [ ] OBTAIN MARRIAGE LICENSE
- [ ] BOOK HAIR STYLIST

- [ ] BOOK NAIL SALON
- [ ] CONFIRM MUSIC SELECTION
- [ ] WRITE VOWS
- [x] PLAN BRIDAL SHOWER
- [ ] PLAN REHEARSAL
- [ ] BOOK REHEARSAL DINNER

- [ ] SHOP FOR WEDDING RINGS
- [ ] PLAN DECORATIONS
- [ ] CHOOSE BOUQUET TYPE
- [ ] FINALIZE GUEST LIST
- [ ] UPDATE PASSPORTS
- [ ] CONFIRM HOTEL ROOMS

Things To Do	Status

TOP PRIORITIES

NOTES & IDEAS

APPOINTMENTS & REMINDERS

Wedding Planner
PLANNING GUIDELINE

4 Months BEFORE WEDDING

April

- [ ] MAIL OUT INVITATIONS
- [ ] MEET WITH OFFICIANT
- [ ] BUY WEDDING FAVORS
- [ ] BUY WEDDING PARTY GIFTS
- [ ] PURCHASE SHOES
- [ ] FINALIZE THANK YOU CARDS

- [ ] FINALIZE HONEYMOON PLANS
- [ ] ATTEND FIRST DRESS FITTING
- [ ] FINALIZE VOWS
- [ ] FINALIZE RECEPTION MENU
- [ ] KEEP TRACK OF RSVPS
- [ ] BOOK PHOTO SESSION

- [ ] CONFIRM CATERER
- [ ] FINALIZE RING FITTING
- [ ] CONFIRM FLOWERS
- [ ] CONFIRM BAND
- [ ] SHOP FOR HONEYMOON
- [ ] BUY GARTER BELT

Things To Do | Status

TOP PRIORITIES

NOTES & IDEAS

APPOINTMENTS & REMINDERS

Notes

My Wedding Planning

WEEK OF: 3/3

WEDDING TO DO LIST

- [ ] Bridal Shower Invites
- [ ] Visit shower venue
- [ ] Down pmt for Merchantile
- [ ] Banner for bridal shower

MONDAY

TUESDAY

WEDNESDAY

THURSDAY

FRIDAY

SATURDAY

APPOINTMENTS & MEETINGS

DATE	TIME	VENDOR	PURPOSE

Weekly Wedding Planning

WEEK OF: _____

MONDAY

TUESDAY

WEDNESDAY

THURSDAY

FRIDAY

SATURDAY

WEDDING TO DO LIST

- [ ]
- [ ]
- [ ]
- [ ]
- [ ]
- [ ]
- [ ]
- [ ]
- [ ]
- [ ]
- [ ]
- [ ]
- [ ]
- [ ]
- [ ]
- [ ]
- [ ]
- [ ]

APPOINTMENTS & MEETINGS

DATE	TIME	VENDOR	PURPOSE

Weekly Wedding Planning

WEEK OF: _____

MONDAY

TUESDAY

WEDNESDAY

THURSDAY

FRIDAY

SATURDAY

WEDDING TO DO LIST

- ☐ _____
- ☐ _____
- ☐ _____
- ☐ _____
- ☐ _____
- ☐ _____
- ☐ _____
- ☐ _____
- ☐ _____
- ☐ _____
- ☐ _____
- ☐ _____
- ☐ _____
- ☐ _____
- ☐ _____
- ☐ _____
- ☐ _____
- ☐ _____

APPOINTMENTS & MEETINGS

DATE	TIME	VENDOR	PURPOSE

Weekly Wedding Planning

WEEK OF: _____

MONDAY

TUESDAY

WEDNESDAY

THURSDAY

FRIDAY

SATURDAY

WEDDING TO DO LIST

- [ ]
- [ ]
- [ ]
- [ ]
- [ ]
- [ ]
- [ ]
- [ ]
- [ ]
- [ ]
- [ ]
- [ ]
- [ ]
- [ ]
- [ ]
- [ ]
- [ ]
- [ ]
- [ ]

APPOINTMENTS & MEETINGS

DATE	TIME	VENDOR	PURPOSE

Weekly Wedding Planning

WEEK OF: _____

MONDAY

TUESDAY

WEDNESDAY

THURSDAY

FRIDAY

SATURDAY

WEDDING TO DO LIST

☐ _____
☐ _____
☐ _____
☐ _____
☐ _____
☐ _____
☐ _____
☐ _____
☐ _____
☐ _____
☐ _____
☐ _____
☐ _____
☐ _____
☐ _____
☐ _____
☐ _____
☐ _____

APPOINTMENTS & MEETINGS

DATE	TIME	VENDOR	PURPOSE

Weekly Wedding Planning

WEEK OF: _____

MONDAY

TUESDAY

WEDNESDAY

THURSDAY

FRIDAY

SATURDAY

WEDDING TO DO LIST

☐ _____
☐ _____
☐ _____
☐ _____
☐ _____
☐ _____
☐ _____
☐ _____
☐ _____
☐ _____
☐ _____
☐ _____
☐ _____
☐ _____
☐ _____
☐ _____
☐ _____
☐ _____

APPOINTMENTS & MEETINGS

DATE	TIME	VENDOR	PURPOSE

Weekly Wedding Planning

WEEK OF: _____

MONDAY

TUESDAY

WEDNESDAY

THURSDAY

FRIDAY

SATURDAY

WEDDING TO DO LIST

APPOINTMENTS & MEETINGS

DATE	TIME	VENDOR	PURPOSE

Weekly Wedding Planning

WEEK OF: _____

MONDAY

TUESDAY

WEDNESDAY

THURSDAY

FRIDAY

SATURDAY

WEDDING TO DO LIST

APPOINTMENTS & MEETINGS

DATE	TIME	VENDOR	PURPOSE

Weekly Wedding Planning

WEEK OF: _____

MONDAY

TUESDAY

WEDNESDAY

THURSDAY

FRIDAY

SATURDAY

WEDDING TO DO LIST

- [ ] _____
- [ ] _____
- [ ] _____
- [ ] _____
- [ ] _____
- [ ] _____
- [ ] _____
- [ ] _____
- [ ] _____
- [ ] _____
- [ ] _____
- [ ] _____
- [ ] _____
- [ ] _____
- [ ] _____
- [ ] _____
- [ ] _____
- [ ] _____

APPOINTMENTS & MEETINGS

DATE	TIME	VENDOR	PURPOSE

Weekly Wedding Planning

WEEK OF: _____

MONDAY

TUESDAY

WEDNESDAY

THURSDAY

FRIDAY

SATURDAY

WEDDING TO DO LIST

APPOINTMENTS & MEETINGS

DATE	TIME	VENDOR	PURPOSE

Weekly Wedding Planning

WEEK OF: _____

MONDAY

TUESDAY

WEDNESDAY

THURSDAY

FRIDAY

SATURDAY

WEDDING TO DO LIST

☐ _____
☐ _____
☐ _____
☐ _____
☐ _____
☐ _____
☐ _____
☐ _____
☐ _____
☐ _____
☐ _____
☐ _____
☐ _____
☐ _____
☐ _____
☐ _____
☐ _____

APPOINTMENTS & MEETINGS

DATE	TIME	VENDOR	PURPOSE

Weekly Wedding Planning

WEEK OF: _____

MONDAY

TUESDAY

WEDNESDAY

THURSDAY

FRIDAY

SATURDAY

WEDDING TO DO LIST

- ☐ _____
- ☐ _____
- ☐ _____
- ☐ _____
- ☐ _____
- ☐ _____
- ☐ _____
- ☐ _____
- ☐ _____
- ☐ _____
- ☐ _____
- ☐ _____
- ☐ _____
- ☐ _____
- ☐ _____
- ☐ _____
- ☐ _____

APPOINTMENTS & MEETINGS

DATE	TIME	VENDOR	PURPOSE

Weekly Wedding Planning

WEEK OF: _____

MONDAY

TUESDAY

WEDNESDAY

THURSDAY

FRIDAY

SATURDAY

WEDDING TO DO LIST

- [ ] _____
- [ ] _____
- [ ] _____
- [ ] _____
- [ ] _____
- [ ] _____
- [ ] _____
- [ ] _____
- [ ] _____
- [ ] _____
- [ ] _____
- [ ] _____
- [ ] _____
- [ ] _____
- [ ] _____
- [ ] _____
- [ ] _____

APPOINTMENTS & MEETINGS

DATE	TIME	VENDOR	PURPOSE

Weekly Wedding Planning

WEEK OF: _____

MONDAY

TUESDAY

WEDNESDAY

THURSDAY

FRIDAY

SATURDAY

WEDDING TO DO LIST

- [ ] _____
- [ ] _____
- [ ] _____
- [ ] _____
- [ ] _____
- [ ] _____
- [ ] _____
- [ ] _____
- [ ] _____
- [ ] _____
- [ ] _____
- [ ] _____
- [ ] _____
- [ ] _____
- [ ] _____
- [ ] _____
- [ ] _____
- [ ] _____

APPOINTMENTS & MEETINGS

DATE	TIME	VENDOR	PURPOSE

Weekly Wedding Planning

WEEK OF: _____

MONDAY

TUESDAY

WEDNESDAY

THURSDAY

FRIDAY

SATURDAY

WEDDING TO DO LIST

☐ _____
☐ _____
☐ _____
☐ _____
☐ _____
☐ _____
☐ _____
☐ _____
☐ _____
☐ _____
☐ _____
☐ _____
☐ _____
☐ _____
☐ _____
☐ _____
☐ _____

APPOINTMENTS & MEETINGS

DATE	TIME	VENDOR	PURPOSE

Weekly Wedding Planning

WEEK OF: _____

Wedding To Do List

- [ ] _____
- [ ] _____
- [ ] _____
- [ ] _____
- [ ] _____
- [ ] _____
- [ ] _____
- [ ] _____
- [ ] _____
- [ ] _____
- [ ] _____
- [ ] _____
- [ ] _____
- [ ] _____
- [ ] _____
- [ ] _____
- [ ] _____

MONDAY

TUESDAY

WEDNESDAY

THURSDAY

FRIDAY

SATURDAY

Appointments & Meetings

DATE	TIME	VENDOR	PURPOSE

Wedding Planner
PLANNING GUIDELINE

1 Month BEFORE WEDDING

- [ ] CHOOSE YOUR MC
- [ ] REQUEST SPECIAL TOASTS
- [ ] ARRANGE TRANSPORTATION
- [ ] CHOOSE YOUR HAIR STYLE
- [ ] CHOOSE YOUR NAIL COLOR
- [ ] ATTEND BRIDAL SHOWER

- [ ] CONFIRM CAKE CHOICES
- [ ] CONFIRM MENU (FINAL)
- [ ] CONFIRM SEATING
- [ ] CONFIRM VIDEOGRAPHER
- [ ] ARRANGE LEGAL DOCS
- [ ] FINALIZE WEDDING DUTIES

- [ ] CONFIRM BRIDESMAID DRESSES
- [ ] MEET WITH DJ/MC
- [ ] FINAL DRESS FITTING
- [ ] WRAP WEDDING PARTY GIFTS
- [ ] CONFIRM FINAL GUEST COUNT
- [ ] CREATE WEDDING SCHEDULE

Things To Do | Status

TOP PRIORITIES

NOTES & IDEAS

APPOINTMENTS & REMINDERS

Weekly Wedding Planning

WEEK OF: _____

MONDAY

TUESDAY

WEDNESDAY

THURSDAY

FRIDAY

SATURDAY

Wedding To Do List

- [ ]
- [ ]
- [ ]
- [ ]
- [ ]
- [ ]
- [ ]
- [ ]
- [ ]
- [ ]
- [ ]
- [ ]
- [ ]
- [ ]
- [ ]
- [ ]
- [ ]
- [ ]

Appointments & Meetings

DATE	TIME	VENDOR	PURPOSE

Weekly Wedding Planning

WEEK OF: _____

MONDAY

TUESDAY

WEDNESDAY

THURSDAY

FRIDAY

SATURDAY

WEDDING TO DO LIST

- [ ]
- [ ]
- [ ]
- [ ]
- [ ]
- [ ]
- [ ]
- [ ]
- [ ]
- [ ]
- [ ]
- [ ]
- [ ]
- [ ]
- [ ]
- [ ]
- [ ]
- [ ]

APPOINTMENTS & MEETINGS

DATE	TIME	VENDOR	PURPOSE

Weekly Wedding Planning

WEEK OF: _____

MONDAY

TUESDAY

WEDNESDAY

THURSDAY

FRIDAY

SATURDAY

WEDDING TO DO LIST

- [ ] _____
- [ ] _____
- [ ] _____
- [ ] _____
- [ ] _____
- [ ] _____
- [ ] _____
- [ ] _____
- [ ] _____
- [ ] _____
- [ ] _____
- [ ] _____
- [ ] _____
- [ ] _____
- [ ] _____
- [ ] _____
- [ ] _____
- [ ] _____

APPOINTMENTS & MEETINGS

DATE	TIME	VENDOR	PURPOSE

Weekly Wedding Planning

WEEK OF: _____

MONDAY

TUESDAY

WEDNESDAY

THURSDAY

FRIDAY

SATURDAY

WEDDING TO DO LIST

- [ ] _____
- [ ] _____
- [ ] _____
- [ ] _____
- [ ] _____
- [ ] _____
- [ ] _____
- [ ] _____
- [ ] _____
- [ ] _____
- [ ] _____
- [ ] _____
- [ ] _____
- [ ] _____
- [ ] _____
- [ ] _____
- [ ] _____

APPOINTMENTS & MEETINGS

DATE	TIME	VENDOR	PURPOSE

Wedding Planner
PLANNING GUIDELINE

1 Week
BEFORE WEDDING

- [ ] PAYMENT TO VENDORS
- [ ] PACK FOR HONEYMOON
- [ ] CONFIRM HOTEL RESERVATION
- [ ] GIVE SCHEDULE TO PARTY
- [ ] DELIVER LICENSE TO OFFICIANT
- [ ] CONFIRM WITH VENDORS

- [ ] PICK UP WEDDING DRESS
- [ ] PICK UP TUXEDOS
- [ ] GIVE MUSIC LIST TO DJ/BAND
- [ ] CONFIRM SHOES/HEELS FIT
- [ ] CONFIRM TRANSPORTATION
- [ ] MONEY FOR GRATUITIES

- [ ] COMPLETE MAKE UP TRIAL
- [ ] CONFIRM RINGS FIT
- [ ] CONFIRM TRAVEL PLANS
- [ ] CONFIRM HOTELS FOR GUESTS
- [ ] OTHER: _____
- [ ] OTHER: _____

Things To Do | Status

TOP PRIORITIES

NOTES & IDEAS

APPOINTMENTS & REMINDERS

Weekly Wedding Planning

WEEK OF: _____

MONDAY

TUESDAY

WEDNESDAY

THURSDAY

FRIDAY

SATURDAY

WEDDING TO DO LIST

- ☐ _____
- ☐ _____
- ☐ _____
- ☐ _____
- ☐ _____
- ☐ _____
- ☐ _____
- ☐ _____
- ☐ _____
- ☐ _____
- ☐ _____
- ☐ _____
- ☐ _____
- ☐ _____
- ☐ _____
- ☐ _____
- ☐ _____

APPOINTMENTS & MEETINGS

DATE	TIME	VENDOR	PURPOSE

Wedding Planner
PLANNING GUIDELINE

1 Day BEFORE WEDDING

- [ ] ATTEND REHEARSAL DINNER
- [ ] FINISH HONEYMOON PACKING
- [ ] GREET OUT OF TOWN GUESTS
- [ ] GET MANICURE/PEDICURE
- [ ] CHECK ON WEDDING VENUE
- [ ] CHECK WEATHER TO PREPARE
- [ ] GIVE GIFTS TO WEDDING PARTY
- [ ] CONFIRM RINGS FIT
- [ ] GET A GOOD NIGHT'S SLEEP

Things To Do | Status

TOP PRIORITIES

NOTES & IDEAS

APPOINTMENTS & REMINDERS

Wedding Day!

Day Of WEDDING

- [ ] GET YOUR HAIR DONE
- [ ] GET YOUR MAKE UP DONE
- [ ] HAVE A LIGHT BREAKFAST
- [ ] MEET WITH BRIDAL PARTY
- [ ] GIVE RINGS TO BEST MAN
- [ ] ENJOY THIS SPECIAL DAY!

Notes

Wedding Guest List

NAME	ADDRESS	PHONE#	# IN PARTY	RSVP ✓

Wedding Guest List

NAME	ADDRESS	PHONE#	# IN PARTY	RSVP ✓

Wedding Guest List

NAME	ADDRESS	PHONE#	# IN PARTY	RSVP ✓

Wedding Guest List

NAME	ADDRESS	PHONE#	# IN PARTY	RSVP ✓

Wedding Guest List

NAME	ADDRESS	PHONE#	# IN PARTY	RSVP ✓

Wedding Guest List

NAME	ADDRESS	PHONE#	# IN PARTY	RSVP ✓

Wedding Guest List

NAME	ADDRESS	PHONE#	# IN PARTY	RSVP ✓

Wedding Guest List

NAME	ADDRESS	PHONE#	# IN PARTY	RSVP ✓

Wedding Guest List

NAME	ADDRESS	PHONE#	# IN PARTY	RSVP ✓

Wedding Guest List

NAME	ADDRESS	PHONE#	# IN PARTY	RSVP ✓

Wedding Guest List

NAME	ADDRESS	PHONE#	# IN PARTY	RSVP ✓

Wedding Guest List

NAME	ADDRESS	PHONE#	# IN PARTY	RSVP ✓

Wedding Guest List

NAME	ADDRESS	PHONE#	# IN PARTY	RSVP ✓

Wedding Guest List

NAME	ADDRESS	PHONE#	# IN PARTY	RSVP ✓

Wedding Seating Chart

Table #

TABLE #:

1:

2:

3:

4:

5:

6:

7:

8:

love

Table #

TABLE #:

1:

2:

3:

4:

5:

6:

7:

8:

Wedding Seating Chart

Table #

TABLE #:
1:
2:
3:
4:
5:
6:
7:
8:

love

Table #

TABLE #:
1:
2:
3:
4:
5:
6:
7:
8:

Wedding Seating Chart

Table #

TABLE #:

1:

2:

3:

4:

5:

6:

7:

8:

Table #

TABLE #:

1:

2:

3:

4:

5:

6:

7:

8:

Wedding Seating Chart

Table #

Table #

TABLE #:
1:
2:
3:
4:
5:
6:
7:
8:

TABLE #:
1:
2:
3:
4:
5:
6:
7:
8:

Wedding Seating Chart

Table #

TABLE #:

1:

2:

3:

4:

5:

6:

7:

8:

Table #

TABLE #:

1:

2:

3:

4:

5:

6:

7:

8:

Wedding Seating Chart

Table #

Table #

TABLE #:
1:
2:
3:
4:
5:
6:
7:
8:

TABLE #:
1:
2:
3:
4:
5:
6:
7:
8:

Wedding Seating Chart

Table #

TABLE #:

1:

2:

3:

4:

5:

6:

7:

8:

Table #

TABLE #:

1:

2:

3:

4:

5:

6:

7:

8:

Wedding Seating Chart

Table #

Table #

TABLE #:
1:
2:
3:
4:
5:
6:
7:
8:

TABLE #:
1:
2:
3:
4:
5:
6:
7:
8:

Wedding Seating Chart

Table #

TABLE #:
1:
2:
3:
4:
5:
6:
7:
8:

Table #

TABLE #:
1:
2:
3:
4:
5:
6:
7:
8:

Wedding Seating Chart

Table #

Table #

TABLE #:

1:

2:

3:

4:

5:

6:

7:

8:

TABLE #:

1:

2:

3:

4:

5:

6:

7:

8:

Wedding Seating Chart

Table #

TABLE #:

1:

2:

3:

4:

5:

6:

7:

8:

Table #

TABLE #:

1:

2:

3:

4:

5:

6:

7:

8:

Wedding Seating Chart

Table #

Table #

TABLE #:
1:
2:
3:
4:
5:
6:
7:
8:

TABLE #:
1:
2:
3:
4:
5:
6:
7:
8:

Wedding Seating Chart

Table #

Table #

TABLE #:

1:

2:

3:

4:

5:

6:

7:

8:

TABLE #:

1:

2:

3:

4:

5:

6:

7:

8:

Wedding Seating Chart

Table #

Table #

TABLE #:
1:
2:
3:
4:
5:
6:
7:
8:

TABLE #:
1:
2:
3:
4:
5:
6:
7:
8:

Wedding Seating Chart

Table #

TABLE #:

1:

2:

3:

4:

5:

6:

7:

8:

Table #

TABLE #:

1:

2:

3:

4:

5:

6:

7:

8:

Wedding Seating Chart

Table #

Table #

TABLE #:

1:

2:

3:

4:

5:

6:

7:

8:

TABLE #:

1:

2:

3:

4:

5:

6:

7:

8:

Wedding Seating Chart

Table #

TABLE #:

1:

2:

3:

4:

5:

6:

7:

8:

Table #

TABLE #:

1:

2:

3:

4:

5:

6:

7:

8:

Wedding Seating Chart

Table #

Table #

TABLE #:
1:
2:
3:
4:
5:
6:
7:
8:

TABLE #:
1:
2:
3:
4:
5:
6:
7:
8:

Wedding Seating Chart

Table #

TABLE #:

1:

2:

3:

4:

5:

6:

7:

8:

Table #

TABLE #:

1:

2:

3:

4:

5:

6:

7:

8:

Wedding Seating Chart

Table #

Table #

TABLE #:
1:
2:
3:
4:
5:
6:
7:
8:

TABLE #:
1:
2:
3:
4:
5:
6:
7:
8:

Wedding Seating Chart

Table #

TABLE #:
1:
2:
3:
4:
5:
6:
7:
8:

Table #

TABLE #:
1:
2:
3:
4:
5:
6:
7:
8:

Wedding Seating Chart

Table #

Table #

TABLE #:

1:

2:

3:

4:

5:

6:

7:

8:

TABLE #:

1:

2:

3:

4:

5:

6:

7:

8:

Wedding Seating Chart

Table #

TABLE #:

1:

2:

3:

4:

5:

6:

7:

8:

Table #

TABLE #:

1:

2:

3:

4:

5:

6:

7:

8:

Wedding Seating Chart

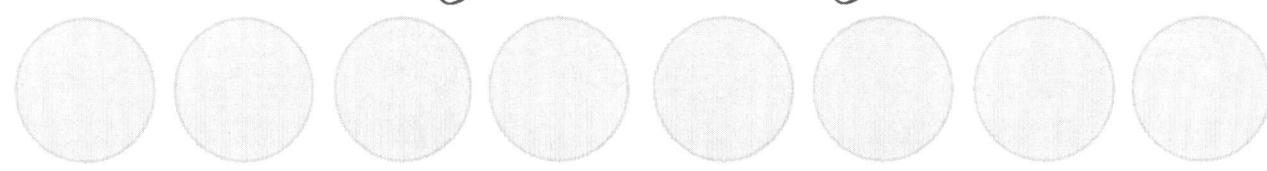

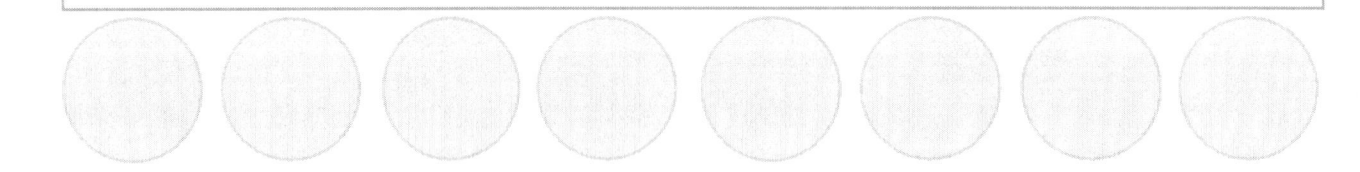

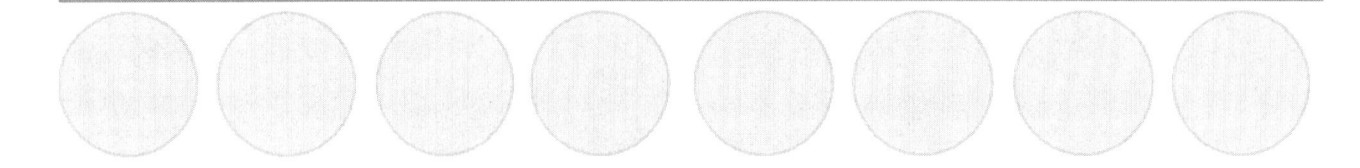

Table #

TABLE #:
| 1: | 2: | 3: | 4: | 5: | 6: | 7: | 8: |
| 9: | 10: | 11: | 12: | 13: | 14: | 15: | 16: |

Table #

TABLE #:
| 1: | 2: | 3: | 4: | 5: | 6: | 7: | 8: |
| 9: | 10: | 11: | 12: | 13: | 14: | 15: | 16: |

Wedding Seating Chart

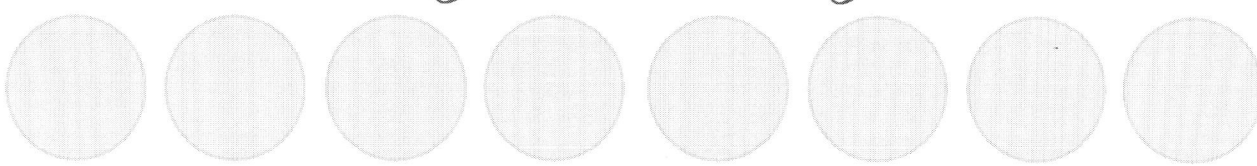

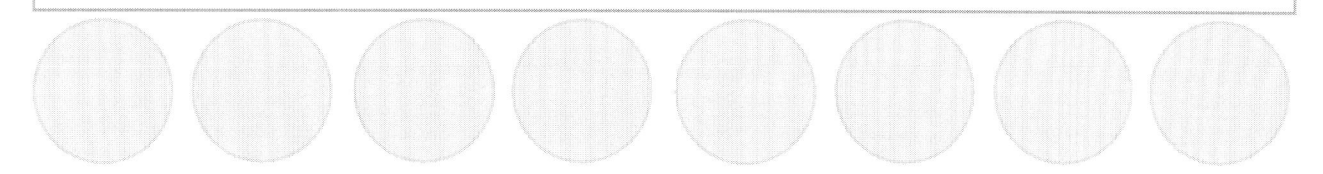

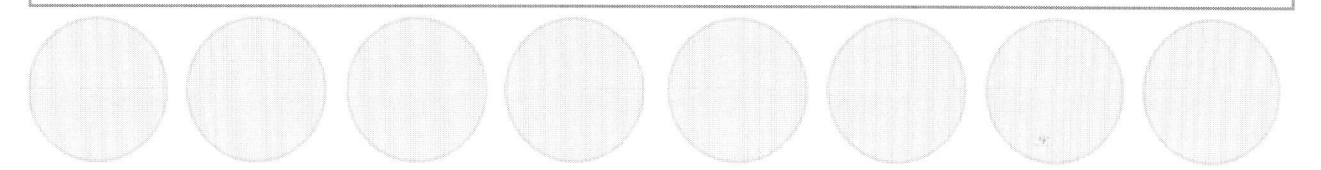

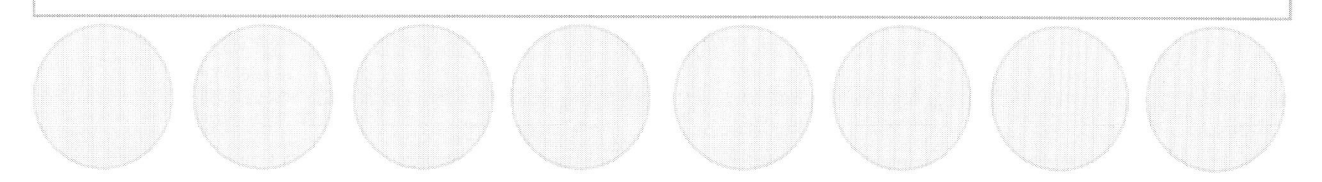

Table #

TABLE #:
| 1: | 2: | 3: | 4: | 5: | 6: | 7: | 8: |
| 9: | 10: | 11: | 12: | 13: | 14: | 15: | 16: |

Table #

TABLE #:
| 1: | 2: | 3: | 4: | 5: | 6: | 7: | 8: |
| 9: | 10: | 11: | 12: | 13: | 14: | 15: | 16: |

Wedding Seating Chart

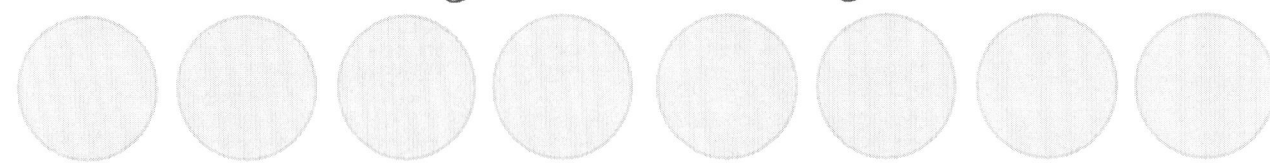

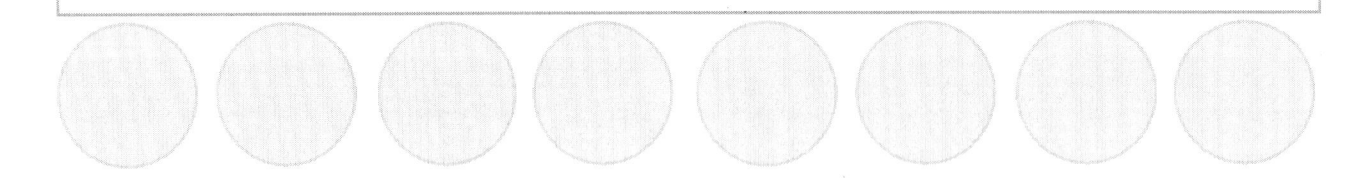

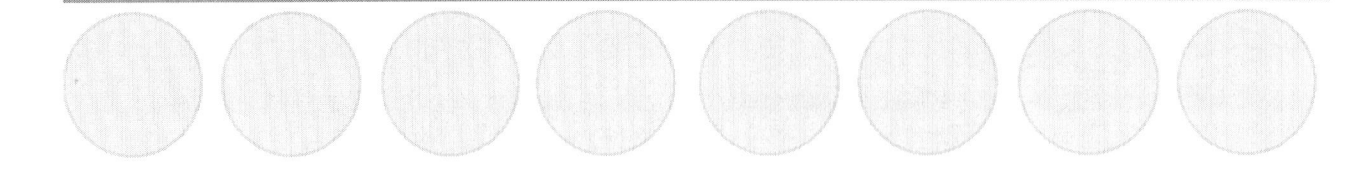

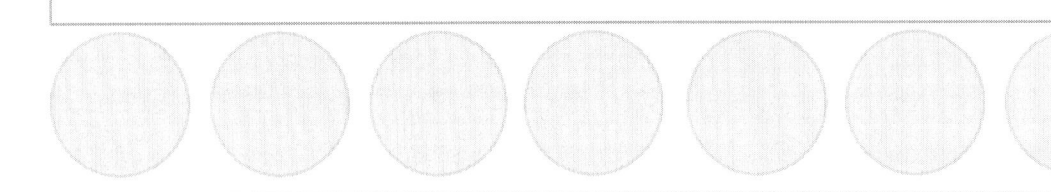

Table #

TABLE #:

| 1: | 2: | 3: | 4: | 5: | 6: | 7: | 8: |
| 9: | 10: | 11: | 12: | 13: | 14: | 15: | 16: |

Table #

TABLE #:

| 1: | 2: | 3: | 4: | 5: | 6: | 7: | 8: |
| 9: | 10: | 11: | 12: | 13: | 14: | 15: | 16: |

Wedding Seating Chart

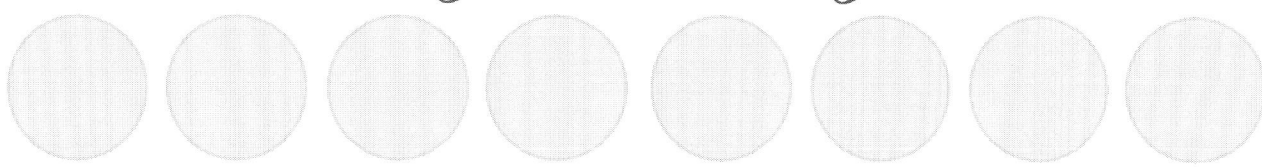

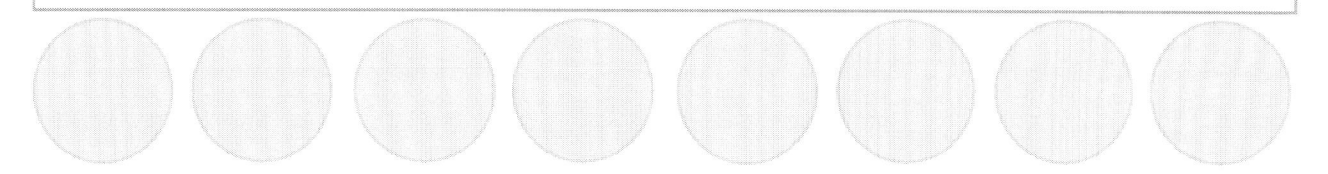

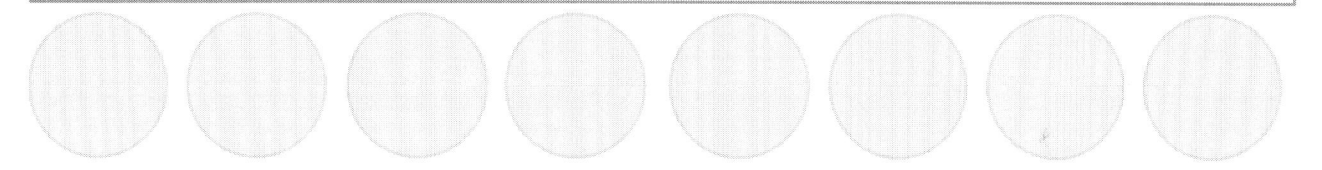

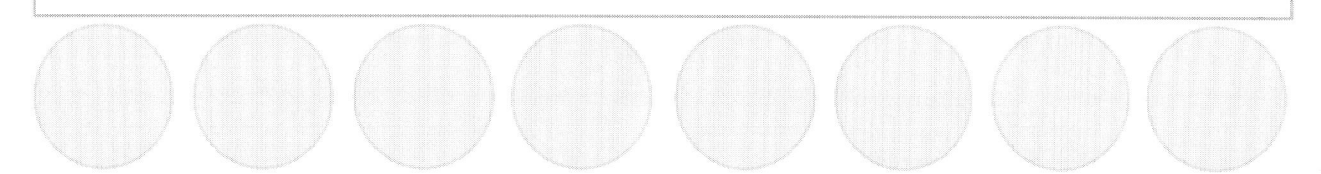

Table #

TABLE #:

| 1: | 2: | 3: | 4: | 5: | 6: | 7: | 8: |
| 9: | 10: | 11: | 12: | 13: | 14: | 15: | 16: |

Table #

TABLE #:

| 1: | 2: | 3: | 4: | 5: | 6: | 7: | 8: |
| 9: | 10: | 11: | 12: | 13: | 14: | 15: | 16: |

Wedding Seating Chart

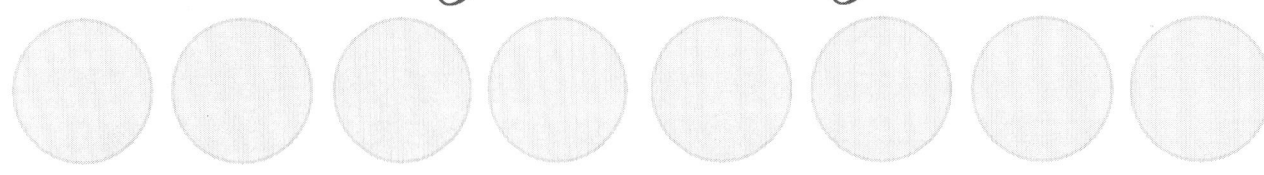

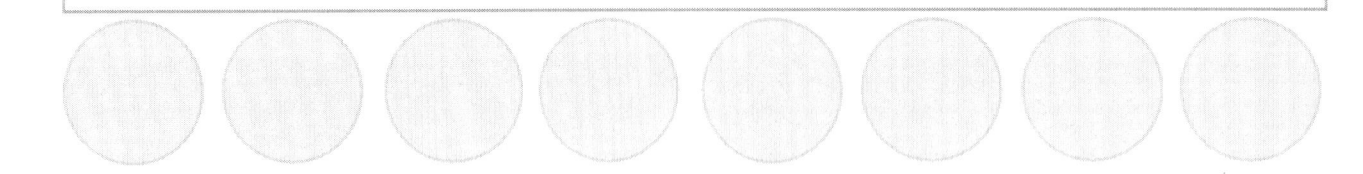

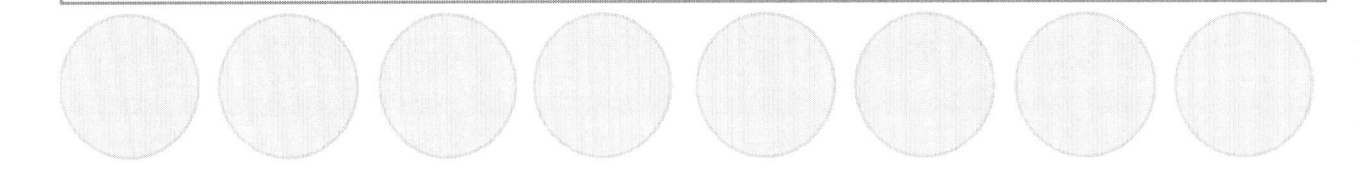

Table

TABLE #:

| 1: | 2: | 3: | 4: | 5: | 6: | 7: | 8: |
| 9: | 10: | 11: | 12: | 13: | 14: | 15: | 16: |

Table

TABLE #:

| 1: | 2: | 3: | 4: | 5: | 6: | 7: | 8: |
| 9: | 10: | 11: | 12: | 13: | 14: | 15: | 16: |

Wedding Seating Chart

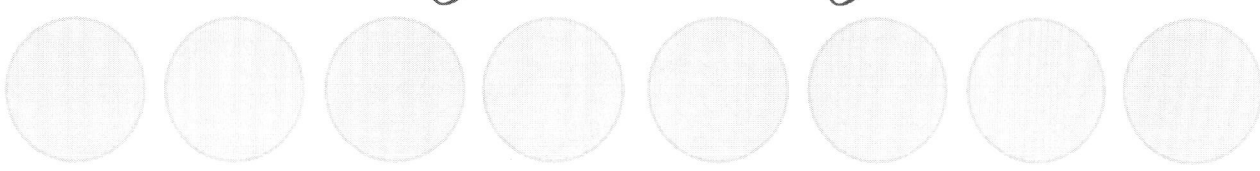

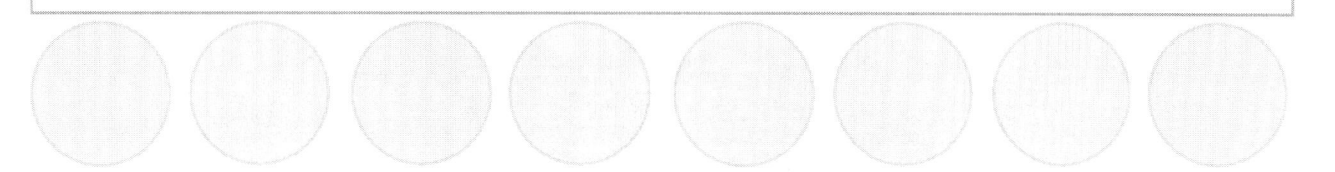

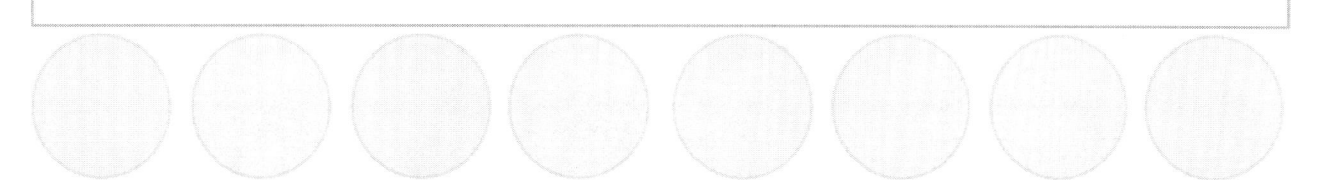

Table #

TABLE #:
1: 2: 3: 4: 5: 6: 7: 8:
9: 10: 11: 12: 13: 14: 15: 16:

Table #

TABLE #:
1: 2: 3: 4: 5: 6: 7: 8:
9: 10: 11: 12: 13: 14: 15: 16:

Love

Best Wishes

Made in the USA
Monee, IL
02 March 2025